Good Deeds

Amy Newmark

CSS

Chicken Soup for the Soul, LLC
Cos Cob, CT

Chicken Soup for the Soul: Good Deeds
Amy Newmark

Published by Chicken Soup for the Soul, LLC www.chickensoup.com

Copyright @2017 by Chicken Soup for the Soul, LLC. All Rights Reserved.

The publisher gratefully acknowledges the many publishers and individuals who granted Chicken Soup for the Soul permission to reprint the cited material.

Front cover illustration courtesy of iStockphoto.com/Mike_Kiev (©Mike_Kiev)

Interior photo of Amy Newmark courtesy of Susan Morrow at SwickPix

Cover and Interior by Daniel Zaccari

ISBN: 978-1-61159-057-9

PRINTED IN THE UNITED STATES OF AMERICA
on acid∞free paper

25 24 23 22 21   04 05 06 07 08 09 10 11

Table of Contents

Some Kind of Miracle

*In this world it is not what we take up, but
what we give up, that makes us rich.*
~Henry Ward Beecher

Her name was Jean. She taught first grade.
She drove a sputtering old Volkswagen
Jetta with dull blue paint and frayed
bucket seats. As a single mother with one young
son, she found that the car served her needs. It
wasn't the speediest vehicle, but Jean was never
late to work. In fact, each school day she was the
first teacher to arrive and the last teacher to leave.

Jean took great care to plan instruction, create
assessments, and decorate her classroom. Parents in
the neighborhood would beat down the principal's

door to have their children assigned to her class. Jean could teach a mouse to read, and all her students passed into second grade with advanced vocabularies and language skills. Needless to say, she was a gifted teacher.

One August, the faculty returned from summer break to see Jean drive up to school with a carload of children. Two sisters in high school had found themselves living in a dangerous environment. They did not want to enter foster care. They asked the caseworker to contact their first grade teacher. Jean lived in a modest home with her son. Yet, she took the sisters in. One of the girls even had a baby. Jean welcomed the baby into her home, too.

Packed with children, the little blue Jetta sputtered onward. Each day, even though Jean took her son and daughters to school and shuttled the baby to daycare, she was still the first teacher in the school parking lot.

During lunch, while faculty members exchanged life stories in the teachers' lounge, Jean never complained about her new responsibilities. She did, however, speak about her car. With three new bodies to transport, the Jetta was too small. It burned oil. Jean needed something new. She wanted a van.

In the teachers' lounge, Jean shared that a new van was not in her budget, especially with three new children in her home. Like a good friend, I listened to her concerns. There was nothing that I could do. At the time, I was a young teacher who lived at home with my mother. I did not have any disposable income. But in my heart I wanted to help Jean purchase a van to accommodate her growing family.

I don't know how the idea came to me. But one day during lunch, I did not go to the teachers' lounge. Instead, I sat at my desk and typed a one-page letter to *The Oprah Winfrey Show*. I shared Jean's story. I told Oprah that Jean was a pillar in our school. Her influence as an educator was so great that two high school girls remembered her kind spirit when they were faced with foster care. They hoped for the impossible and they got it — their first grade teacher welcomed them into her home. And though her resources were limited, Jean made sacrifices to care for the girls as if they were her own.

A month passed. One morning the principal called Jean into his office. He wanted her to attend a "teachers' conference" in Chicago. She had two days to pack. Jean made arrangements for childcare and flew to the Windy City. A limousine driver dashed her away to Harpo Studios for a surprise taping of *The Oprah Winfrey Show*.

Oprah's topic for that day was generosity. Midway through the taping, she called Jean to the stage. Oprah hugged the dedicated teacher and explained she had received a letter expressing her need for a van. The audience listened to the details of Jean's story and clapped for her. Then Oprah announced that Jean would receive a new Chrysler van for her family. Cheers filled the studio and Jean trembled with disbelief. She was speechless, but her tears expressed her overwhelming gratitude.

The year was 1999. Six hundred miles away, I watched the joy of it all from the television in my living room. Jean's big heart taught me many lessons that year. I learned that as we satisfy the needs of others, God supplies our needs. I learned that the simplest acts (like writing a letter) can require a daring faith. And nothing is impossible. Miracles happen every day.

~Alice Faye Duncan

Finding Peace

All God's angels come to us disguised.
~James Russell Lowell

I heard her tiny body hit the wall before he slammed shut the bathroom door. She sounded more like a child than an eight-pound dog when she cried out. That sound pierced the wall that separated us. On the other side, my heart was pounding in terror.

My stalker was inside my home, raping me. And all I could hear was my heartbeat, his rancid breathing, and my little dog's sudden silence.

I was bleeding from places on my body I could no longer feel. She was whimpering, in the soft delicate way she had whimpered when we first met.

I had rescued her from the colorful alleyways of Venice Beach, on a Sunday evening vibrant with music, laughter, and the other sounds — those of discontent — that fill Los Angeles after dark. She was curled up in a shadowy corner, lying atop discarded debris and broken glass, ignored and alone.

At first I thought she was a large rodent, but it was her huge ears that drew me closer. I saw that she was a tiny dog, trembling from her infected wounds, the worms that had invaded her empty belly, and, most of all — fear.

Had I not found her when I did she would have died right there in that rat-infested alley. Had I not found her when I did, I would have died too — of sadness, self-loathing, and the bondage of memory that kept me prisoner. It was destiny. We were waiting to find each other.

After she recovered at the local vet, she came home to me. The first few months were challenging. She hid beneath my bedroom dresser, never allowing me to touch or cuddle her in any way. I simply slipped a bowl of water and kibble in front of her hiding place each morning, and opened the French doors that led to my gated yard for her to relieve herself. I was content to know that she was safe. It was enough that she had a home, that she was loved, and that she had given me both a challenge and a purpose.

That frightened little dog was a mirror to my brokenness. I understood her lack of trust. I had stopped trusting too after I walked in on my husband naked in the bathtub with the babysitter. I hid from intimacy in darker places than she could ever squeeze her tiny body into.

But one day, after months of hiding, I woke to find her on the pillow next to my own. From that day forward, we were inseparable, until my rapist ripped us apart.

He had a tattoo on his hand of an Om. Ironic, because I had named her Om Shanti. "Om" is a vibration often defined as the sound of creation. And "Shanti" means "peace."

For years we clung to one another. She was my very best friend. She was the only living being who truly saw me, and still cared, without pretense, when I walked into a room. She was the pulsating-with-life reflection of God that I trusted with all of me. She was the wag at the door that welcomed me after long days, and her smile at the end of the leash reminded me that life was still unfolding outside my home and outside my head. She was the friend who licked my tears when life demanded more than I had to give.

When the ambulance arrived, Shanti was freed from the bathroom. The policeman who found her said she was too swift; he tried to catch her but could not. The front door had been left open, and Shanti was last seen chasing behind the ambulance that carried me away on the busy streets of Los Angeles.

When I finally was released from the hospital I spent each waking moment posting signs outside and online in search of my best friend. I couldn't breathe without her, couldn't heal, and couldn't sleep.

A month or so went by and I had given up hope of ever seeing her again. I was pulled from a sedated sleep when the phone rang. It was a woman from Boston, 3,000 miles away, who just so happened to be going through missing pet announcements when she read my story. She said the mental image of this poor rescued dog chasing an ambulance led her to call and that she felt compelled to help me search. Her name, she said, was Angel.

One week later Angel called again. "I don't know if it's your Shanti," she said, "but there is a dog with the same huge ears wearing the red collar you described, but without any tags, in a kennel in the city of Downey." Downey was 150 miles from my home. Although I knew it was an impossibility, there was something in the spirit of her voice that gave me hope — that restored a semblance of my faith and propelled me to drive the distance.

I walked into the kennel shaking, and handed the flier and pictures of Shanti to the woman behind the desk.

"There's a dog here that fits this description," she said. "A nurse from a hospital in Los Angeles found her hiding under a bush. But apparently she was headed out here that night, so she brought the dog with her and dropped her off the next morning. If you'll follow me, I can take you back to her. I do hope she's yours. The poor thing is scheduled to be put down by end of day."

As I turned the corner I heard her yelping with excitement. It was her! It was Shanti. I had found her 150 miles from home. She jumped into my arms and I fell onto the floor. She was climbing on my head, wagging every part of her body, and I was laughing and crying at the very same time. We had rescued each other again. And we had both survived to love another day.

The drive home was the very first time I truly exhaled since the trauma. I cried out in gratitude and awe to God until I reached my front door. I immediately ran to the phone to call Angel. When I dialed her number, the automated response said,

"The number you have dialed is a non-working number; please check the number and dial again."

~Piper M. Dellums

Room for a Turkey

Genuine kindness is no ordinary act,
but a gift of rare beauty.
~Sylvia Rossetti

I was brushing my teeth getting ready for bed when the phone rang. *This cannot be good*, I thought as I hurried to see why I was summoned so late at night. My mind quickly ran through the list of family members that might need my help, but the voice on the other end of the line was only vaguely familiar.

"Lindy, this is Leslie," she said. "I hope I didn't catch you sleeping."

I didn't know Leslie very well, so I was a bit dumbfounded that she would be calling me at eleven o'clock at night. We had children of similar ages and occasionally spoke with each other at various community events, but to say we were friends was a stretch. I assured her that I was still up and asked what she needed. I was afraid it might be something really dire to cause her to reach out to someone she barely knew. Instead, she asked me a most peculiar question.

"Do you have room for a turkey in your freezer?" she asked.

We had lots of room in our freezer. In fact, we had too much room. My husband's business had taken a downturn and we were pretty much at the bottom of our food supply.

"Sure," I responded, "Did your freezer break down?"

"Not exactly," Leslie replied, "but if you will give me directions to your house I will explain when I get there."

This was certainly odd. I told my husband that Leslie was coming over and needed to use our freezer.

"Our freezer? Now?" Tom asked. "We hardly know her." I didn't have an explanation for him, so I just shrugged my shoulders.

We quickly changed back into blue jeans from our nightclothes and scurried to meet her outside so the doorbell would not wake our four children.

Pulling up the driveway was a huge freezer truck. Leslie stepped down from the passenger side and explained that her husband serviced a small grocery store that had just lost its lease. They had to empty all the freezers before midnight that night. Leslie and her husband thought it was a shame to just throw all this good food into a Dumpster so she began to go through her list of contacts, dropping off food to anyone she could think of who might be willing to take it.

When she put the turkey in our freezer Leslie noticed that it was pretty empty. "Is it okay if we just fill this up?" she asked. "We have a few more turkeys and some other items." Ours was the last place they planned to stop and anything left would have to be discarded.

While Leslie's husband was bringing in a load of food he noticed a smaller freezer that we also had in the garage. "If that works," he said, pointing to the freezer we had planned to donate, "plug it in and we can fill that, too!"

The four of us walked back and forth between the truck and our freezers carrying armloads of frozen foods. In less than an hour we had filled both freezers in the garage and even the small freezer space in our refrigerator inside the house!

Still not fully understanding what had just occurred, I asked her, "When will you be coming back for all this?"

Leslie just laughed. She rearranged the blocks of food for extra space and wedged one last Butterball in place. Then she shut the freezer door and wiped the frost from her hands. When she turned to face me she replied, "We don't want it back. It is yours to eat, to share, to enjoy! We have been delivering food since 5:00 p.m. and have exhausted our list of contacts. That's the end of it! Thanks for helping us out." Then she and her husband climbed back into their truck, waved goodbye and backed down the driveway.

"For helping *them* out?" I said out loud. Tom and I watched them drive away and then just looked at one another. What had just happened didn't seem real. Even though it was midnight, we were compelled to go back into the garage and look in the freezers. We opened one freezer door and counted four big frozen turkeys. In the other freezer there were three more. Stacked around them were pizzas and freezer meals, vegetables and desserts. These were the expensive, convenient foods that we never bought but often longed to try. Our freezers were so full there was no space left, not even for an ice cream bar!

Leslie had no idea that we were in such a tight financial spot that we struggled to buy groceries. It was not something that Tom or I shared with anyone. My eyes filled with tears because I knew that God had heard the concerns of my heart and was meeting our needs in a miraculous, surprising way. Having plenty of food for my family was a huge stress reliever during a difficult time.

Over the next several months we ate well and shared turkey with friends, family and neighbors. By the time the freezer food finally ran out we were back on our feet. Our income had surged and buying groceries was no longer a problem. We blessed someone else with our now empty extra freezer.

I admit that I still startle at late night calls, assuming the worst, but then I remember that summer night when an acquaintance called. She had a smile in her voice when she asked, "Do you have room for a turkey?"

~Lindy Schneider

Miracle Mike

*There are two ways to live: you can live as if
nothing is a miracle; you can live
as if everything is a miracle.*
~Albert Einstein

"Stop worrying, Dad! The car is *fine*. I'm going!" Famous last words from a stubborn eighteen-year-old version of myself as I flew out the door to go to my first college party.

The year was 1996 and I was just finishing up my first semester of community college. I had opted to get the first two years of general education classes under my belt at the more affordable community college before transferring to a university in my junior year. The closest community college was thirty minutes away, so I lived at home with my dad and commuted. Thus, since a commute was going to be involved, I had to have a car. After a few months of borrowing my dad's vehicle, we had finally decided it was time for me to own my very first car.

I was frugal (and so was my family) so we headed straight to the used car section. I found what I thought was a great deal on a cute little car, but my dad had his doubts from the start. He wanted to get it thoroughly checked out before we agreed to purchase it, but not me. I was in a hurry.

"Daaaad. We can't give every car the third degree. Let's just pick one already. I want *this* one…"

So, he gave in. Yes! The cute little car was mine!

And no sooner had we driven off the lot than the problems started. First, the constant overheating. Next, the knocking sound coming from the engine. But oh no — I was not to be deterred. Not Miss Fancy Pants College Girl. I had my own car!

So, the needle went to the "H" every now and then? Big deal! I just wouldn't look at it. So, there was a pesky little sound coming from the engine? Hey — I could just turn up the radio. Problem solved!

So, here I was, smack in the middle of ignoring a multitude of warnings, heading out the door to a Friday night party in my college town. I had been looking forward to it for weeks and had been shocked that my dad was allowing me to go. But as the night arrived, along with an unexpected winter snowstorm, my dad started having second thoughts. The snowy roads combined with the problems that were plaguing my car were enough to make him speak up. But I was not listening. I was an *adult*, thank you very much. I was not about to miss that party.

So, off I went.

I swung by and picked up my friend Carrie and the two of us started on our thirty-minute drive in the snow. Just as we hit a long stretch of somewhat deserted highway, the inevitable finally happened.

My precious little cute car spit and sputtered its final breath... and died. Luckily, I had just enough time to coast to the side of the highway, just barely over the line onto the shoulder, before it came to a complete stop. And there we were. Two eighteen-year-old girls stranded on the side of the road on a snowy dark night. Now, remember, this was 1996 — this was before we all had cell phones. There was no whipping out the cell and calling Dad for help. No, we were stuck. Really, really stuck.

We started looking around to see if there were any houses nearby. Of course it was too dark to see anyway, but having driven this stretch of road so many times in the past few months, we knew that we had managed to break down in the least inhabited portion of the drive. Walking to get help was not going to be an option. So, we decided to do the only thing we knew to do. We got out of the car and started trying to wave down passing cars.

After having no luck whatsoever, and starting to freeze in the frigid temperatures, we piled back into the car. We hadn't sat there long before — oddly — a truck pulled over to the side of the road in front of us. Looking back, it never occurred to me how strange it was that he knew to stop. We were no longer standing outside the car and there were obviously no lights on inside the car since everything had stopped working. How did he even know there were people in the car needing help? Regardless, there he was. And boy, were we grateful.

Of course, we were hesitant at first to climb into a stranger's truck. At this point, however, we were cold and desperate. The warmth of the truck was too inviting to pass up. As we climbed inside, the first thing we noticed was a picture of what we assumed to be his beautiful wife and two smiling kids taped to his dashboard.

He introduced himself as "Mike" and asked where we were headed. We explained our situation and where we were headed and, as luck would have it, he was heading that very way and would be glad to drop us off. We felt immediately at ease with

Mike. He had a jolly laugh and had us giggling along with his family stories by the time we arrived at our destination. As we piled out of the car, we asked Mike if there was anything we could do to repay him. His only answer? "Just be careful, girls. Listen to your dad next time." And with a wink, he drove away.

Had I told him that my dad had told me not to drive that night? I couldn't remember. I didn't think I had… but surely I must have. How else would he have known? I shook off the thought, and headed in to the party. I made the dreaded call to my father to explain the situation. Since it was so late and travel was so treacherous, we decided to stay at our host's house for the night. My dad would pick us up in the morning when the weather had cleared. In the meantime, he would call the tow truck and have the car removed from the highway.

The next morning, my dad picked us up and we drove to the tow lot to get some personal belongings from the car. As we pulled into the snow-covered lot and rounded a curve, my jaw dropped open. I couldn't believe what I was seeing. There, under a thin layer of new snow, sat my car.

Demolished.

I was floored. What? What had happened? My father gave me "the look," to which I immediately responded, "I didn't do that, Daddy! It didn't look like that when I left it, I promise!"

Of course, I was wasting my breath telling him that. Obviously, anyone could see that I hadn't been in the car. Why is that? Well, for one thing, the driver's side was smashed in. You couldn't even see the steering wheel anymore — it was hidden beneath a mangled pile of metal that used to be my precious little cute car.

After a few phone calls and information from the tow truck driver, we learned that after Mike picked us up off of the side of the road, a driver had fallen asleep behind the wheel of a U-Haul truck, veered off the road, and smashed into my car, totaling it. The U-Haul driver, seeing that no one was in the car and realizing that his own vehicle was still in good driving condition, drove on and stopped later down the road to call in the incident. And here's the kicker. After a review of the police report and the U-Haul driver's statement, the estimated time of impact was able to be determined. The time? Approximately two minutes after Mike had picked us up off the highway.

Two minutes.

A mere two minutes later and my friend and I would have been sitting huddled in that car trying to keep warm as the U-Haul plowed into us. There is no doubt in my mind that we would have not survived the impact.

After discovering what happened, Carrie and I asked around to try to find Mike. We described his vehicle to everyone we knew. We even paid for a small ad to be placed in the newspaper asking him to come forward so that we could give him our proper thanks. No one ever turned up.

No one had ever heard of Mike.

I sit here eighteen years later reflecting on that night and I wonder. Somewhere down deep inside, I do believe in miracles.

And I'm certain my Mike was one of them.

~Melissa Edmondson

One Small Gesture Can Reap Huge Blessings

For it is in the giving that we receive.
~Saint Francis of Assisi

n more than one occasion I have pulled up to the drive-through window at Starbucks and the cashier has said, "No charge! The person in front of you is 'paying it forward.'" What a nice way to start the day. I always wish I could run after that person to thank him or her.

Consequently, I always watch my rearview mirror

to see if someone I deem "worthy" of that gesture is behind me. Once in a while I do, and I feel like a naughty schoolgirl who just got away with something when I pay for their coffee. I trust my generosity is appreciated although that is not why I do it. Giving in secret is much more rewarding—and fun!

That particular morning, I glanced in my rearview mirror when I got to the drive-through window to pay. An attractive middle-aged woman was driving a shiny sports car with the top down. I could see her gold jewelry glistening in the sunshine. I smiled to myself thinking, *No way does she need me to buy her coffee!* I imagined she had more money than she knew what to do with, but then that voice shouted in my heart: *Pay for her coffee.*

Are you kidding me? I shouldn't have been buying a special coffee for myself, let alone a stranger. My finances were tight and I was already feeling guilty for spending cash on my *own* coffee.

I cringed, but I told the cashier, "Please put the red convertible's order on my tab." As soon as I said it, I felt relief. I knew I had been obedient to that little voice and that was all that really mattered. I paid the server and proceeded to the parking lot. I had a quick errand to run. When I got back to my car, the red convertible was parked next to mine.

"Hi," the lady said. She was gorgeous and reeked of money. "I want to thank you for the coffee this morning. I never expected that."

"You're welcome. I was just 'paying it forward.'" I smiled and started to get into my car.

"Do you have a minute?" she asked.

I nodded and she proceeded to cry. "I don't know why I am telling you this but I need you to know how much I appreciate that cup of coffee this morning."

"There's no need to thank me. I was happy to do it." I felt a twinge of guilt, as I wasn't being totally honest.

"My husband and I may have to declare bankruptcy. Our business partner swindled us out of all our holdings and left us in the cold. This could not have come at a worse time as we lost our son to cancer last month. He was only twenty-six years old. Our hearts are breaking and we aren't thinking clearly. I blamed God and asked Him why He didn't care. I told him it was not fair and there were moments when I didn't know if I could go on. I needed a sign that He still loved us and that everything would work out. When you bought my coffee this morning, I knew that was my sign. I had no idea God cared enough to tell a stranger to buy my coffee. Thank you ever so much. I will never forget this, especially if I am feeling alone."

Now I was the one who was fighting back tears. I told her that I could relate on both counts. We, too, had recently lost our son, and we had also lost our business to partners who stole it from us. I shared how God does indeed care and He would mend her broken heart.

We chatted for a few more minutes, exchanged phone numbers and set up a coffee date.

I sat in my car for a few minutes, visibly

shaken. I believe I gave her much more than a cup of coffee that morning. I will be her friend and her confidante. I will lend support — she will know she is not alone.

Next time I am in the drive-through and feel the urge to pay it forward — there will be no hesitation.

~Carol Graham

The Journey
Back from Gone

*Hope is the companion of power, and mother
of success; for who so hopes strongly has
within him the gift of miracles.*
~Samuel Smiles

I happily snacked on a rare Lunchables between
the two sets of sliding doors at Kmart, trying
to stay warm. My black fake leather coat and
spiked hair didn't do much to keep me warm in
the Michigan blizzard, but I wasn't allowed to
go back to the homeless shelter until 5:00 p.m.
I hunkered down so the store manager wouldn't
see me as she passed; she knew I was a homeless

teen trying to keep warm and would call security to shoo me away.

There had been a time when I was a privileged boarding school student, and for all appearances, I had everything going for me. Beneath my family's smiling Christmas card, though, lay abuse, fear and control. When I graduated high school, my father put me in a Catholic seminary to keep track of me. Too afraid to defy him, I began classes in the seminary he chose. On the second weekend, I had my first drink, then was drugged and raped. After my discharge from the hospital, the school asked me to withdraw.

I had no other choice. I flew home.

That Halloween, I mustered up the courage to tell my father what had been done to me. He played with his fingers, not looking at me as I wept, recounting as much detail as I could so he understood it wasn't my fault. His expression was inscrutable. After I finished delivering my message, there was a long pause before he spoke.

"Let me get this straight. As of right now, you have run away from home, picked up smoking of all things, drank alcohol and now you've slept around? You have screwed up your life in every way except using drugs, but I suppose you'll go for that, too, soon enough."

He kicked me out. Numbly, I found an apartment on the crime-ridden side of town. Eventually, I met the neighbors, who were hardened addicts. My drug use with them escalated into a full-blown addict lifestyle in less than a month. "I'm too far gone," I would tell myself any time someone told me I needed to fix my shattered life.

After nearly a year of silencing my pain and rage with every substance I could hustle into my body, I experienced a miracle. Lying on a filthy couch in front of the television with a newly emptied needle playing between my fingers, a children's services commercial began. A parade of children excitedly told the camera what they wanted to be when they grew up. Confused by the high, I waited for my turn to announce what I wanted to do. Dark panic crept across my heart as I realized I didn't remember what career or life goals I'd had. The realization sobered me quickly from my high and I began to plan.

I decided to join the military. When I told my parents, they chuckled at me. I quit drugs cold turkey and my new hope tempered the withdrawal. My roommates, however, grew concerned that I would soon be an informant and threw me out with only a sad little backpack containing two changes of clothes. All at once, I was a homeless teen addict with little more than a wisp of hope.

I checked into a homeless shelter after begging my father fruitlessly for help. He had laughed again, enjoying the moment and telling me I would never survive on my own. For years, his derisive chortles would fuel me to push through the months of rape, beatings and sometimes starvation following that final conversation with him.

As I sat, content to warm myself and eat my Lunchables in the safety of Kmart, a woman dressed in a long, teal coat stopped by on her way out of the store.

"Have you had anything real to eat? You're so thin. Let me get you something better than that."

It was the first time I'd been spoken to with kindness in years, and I nearly fell out of the handicap cart I was occupying. The manager spotted me and came over.

"I told you to leave! Unless you are buying something, you can't loiter here. Next time I see you, I am calling the cops."

I was too ashamed of my clearly homeless state to accept the kind woman's offer so I quickly scrambled out into the blizzard. Out of the corner of my eye, I saw a gang member waiting by a corner to jump me. I doubled back and took her hand.

I don't remember her name, but that woman changed my life. She ignored the stares from all sides as she led me to a table in a nice restaurant. She asked me about my passions and goals, and when I told her I was trying to join the Air Force, her face split into a warm smile. She believed in me; beyond my spiked hair, cheap hoop earrings and the piece of string I utilized as a belt, she saw potential. "Maybe I'm not actually too far gone." I thought. The realization was as fresh and life-giving as each course she ordered for us.

The moment we stepped out of the restaurant, the sounds of honking cars coupled with shouts from the alley grounded me. I fell from cloud nine and the dignity I had gained smashed onto the sidewalk. Suddenly full of shame, I fled. I never saw her again.

The mysterious woman had given me a new addiction: hope. For the next two months, I coordinated with a recruiter and went through military enlistment processing.

In April 2010, I left for basic. I went through rigorous counseling and physical training, but the most powerful transformation was left on my growing heart by a parade of one soul after the next, tossing love into the abyss of my self-worth with the same message: "You're not too far gone."

The love that was heaped into me over the years began to spill over; finally I had an abundance to share as well. I began to teach life skills classes to homeless teens. On occasion, friends would ask me how my heart could handle seeing so much brokenness and despair. "No one is too far gone" had become my mantra.

Six months ago, I decided I wanted a bag of Fritos. Locking up my house, I hopped in my car and rolled to the corner store. What I found changed my life.

The cashier, who was trying to sell a teen girl, panicked and asked if I could take his "friend" to the homeless clinic. She was collapsed on the floor by the register. Not comprehending the situation, I asked the girl if she was all right. Her clothes were caked stiff in filth and bodily fluids. In spite of the meth sores encircling her lips, she looked to be around fifteen years old.

I packed her into my car, assessing the situation. She was too ill to go to the clinic, I decided. She introduced herself as Paloma before passing out. I rushed her to the hospital.

For the sake of her privacy I will say only this: Statistically, she should have died from the profound abuse that made her so ill. I lived with her in the hospital for a week. As she improved, word spread and soon she had a stream of visitors, filling the holes in her heart with love. They joked with her, played with her hair and supplied her with clothing sporting her favorite bands. During her last night in the hospital, I kissed her goodnight on the forehead and turned to leave for the evening. Her sweet voice piped up: "Night Mom. I love you."

Paloma is now my daughter because I know no one is beyond hope. I placed her in a nearby transition home where she has counseling and tutoring to help her learn to read and write. She loves to play with our puppy and cranks the car radio with the same smile as any other kid. Last month, as we drove to a hiking trail, she filled me in on the latest drama with her new friends. One of the friends she described made me nervous, and I worried she would cause trouble for Paloma. Cautiously I asked her if she felt the girl would do well in the home. Her smiling answer, for the hundredth time in my life rocked my world: "Mom, no one is too far gone."

~Skye Galvas

Future Restored

Love and kindness are never wasted.
They always make a difference.
They bless the one who receives them,
and they bless you, the giver.
~Barbara de Angelis

My pillow was saturated in tears that winter night. An e-mail from my college's financial aid office was still showing on my computer screen. I did not have the money to return the next semester.

My roommates were comparing their new class schedules, strategizing how to share textbooks, and calculating nap schedules into their new class line up. They were another step closer to their dreams.

I was packing *my* dreams into boxes, along with blankets, pillows and towels. My dad helped load my belongings into his faded blue pickup truck and I hugged my friends goodbye. There were a mixture of well wishes and hopes for my return, but I was confronting the prospect that my departure was permanent.

As the New Year passed, my social networks were filled with my friends' hopes for the school season. They were returning to school and I was at home. I didn't realize how lonely it would feel.

It was the first official day of classes. I woke to the ring of the phone downstairs. As my father talked on the phone, I started searching for jobs in my area. Now that I wasn't in school, I would need to start paying back my school loans.

The fact that I would not be returning to school became real. Ever since I had packed my things, there had been this small hope that maybe something miraculous would happen. But as I searched the job listings, I knew it was because I had given up hope.

No hero was going to swoop in and save the day.

The clunk of the phone being hastily placed into the receiver and the thundering of my dad's footsteps pulled me from my self-pity.

"Pack up your stuff, you're heading back to school!"

My father's face was flushed as he grabbed a suitcase.

"That was the financial aid office. Someone donated $5,000 and paid the remainder of your spring tuition."

"But Dad, I'm not signed up for any classes!"

A big boyish grin spread on my dad's face.

"Your professors have made room for you. Your first day of class is today. Now get your stuff packed, we gotta move!"

In the ensuing chaos of throwing an assortment of clothes, bedding, and shower needs back into the pale blue pickup truck, my dad explained that the donor was unknown and had just paid off my tuition that morning. My professors had been notified and made a schedule so I could continue to graduate on time. I called my roommates and they cheered and said they would get my side of the room cleared and ready for my arrival.

It wasn't until I was sitting in my first class three hours later, with the pen and notebook we had bought at a gas station on the drive back to school, that I realized that I was actually back. The miracle I thought wouldn't come... came. It was just a little late getting here.

I never learned who paid for my return, but whoever you are, you were my miracle. Thank you.

~Nan Rockey

The Gift Card

*Help one another; there's no time like the
present and no present like the time.*
~James Durst

The year 2014 had been financially difficult for me. Aside from social security, my
only other source of income was writing.
During the last six months of the year, several of
my manuscripts had been rejected and the idea
well was running dry. I suffered a series of health
problems; my twelve-year-old car needed a new
battery, tires and brakes; the water heater and
furnace both quit working; Christmas was just
around the corner and my checking account was
looking alarmingly anemic. Upon opening one

of my Christmas cards, I discovered a gift card along with the note: "Buy something special for yourself."

There was no signature on the card nor return address on the envelope. All of a sudden, ideas began pouring into my head. I could buy a new pair of winter boots, a digital camera or that printer I'd been needing. Maybe I'd buy some of the DVDs I'd been wanting. Wow... this would MAKE my Christmas. Feeling both pleased and oddly embarrassed, I set the card aside until I could figure out who might have sent it.

Along with several other organizations, our church sponsors a food pantry. Local grocery stores provide bread, cereal, eggs, beans, canned goods and produce. Once people register, they can come in and take whatever they need. Everything is free. As I was helping distribute food two weeks before Christmas, I noticed a forlorn-looking woman approaching my counter. She wore a stained T-shirt, threadbare jeans and a denim jacket that showed signs of recent mending. As she placed a bag of dried pinto beans and a small onion into a plastic grocery store bag, I asked if she was shopping for her family.

"No," she replied, "just me." There was obvious sadness in her voice but also a need to tell someone her troubles. "My daughter and her family live in Florida and my husband died a couple of months ago. I was thinking that maybe I'd get some tortillas and beans for Christmas dinner. My husband always liked pintos."

"What was his name?" I asked.

"Jack." She started telling me all about her husband: his crooked smile, the color of his eyes, the years he spent driving a big rig to support the family and the way he enjoyed going to church, especially on Christmas Eve. As she spoke, tears trickled down her cheeks. "This will be my first Christmas without him. We never had a lot of money but now there isn't even enough to buy our grandchildren Christmas gifts."

Searching in my apron pocket for a tissue, I

discovered the gift card and handed it to her, saying, "Here — maybe this will help — Merry Christmas."

At the New Years' service, our pastor read the following letter forwarded to him by the food pantry:

Dear friends at the food pantry,

Two weeks ago, I felt as if life wasn't worth living. My husband, Jack, drove an 18-wheeler for a living. On his way home from Colorado three months ago, he ran into a sudden rainstorm on the Interstate. The driver in the car in front of him lost control on the slick pavement and started swerving from lane to lane. In order to avoid hitting the car, Jack drove his truck into a ditch. It overturned and he was killed. I later learned that the people in the car, a mom, a dad and a two-month-old baby, were on their way to visit family in Texas. Jack saved them all.

I was devastated. In all our twenty-three years of marriage, Jack had never wanted me to work. After his death, I tried to find work but, without skills, no one wanted to hire me. When what little money I had left after burying Jack ran out, I started going to the food pantry. Two weeks before Christmas, I came to buy the ingredients for what I thought might be my last dinner — pinto beans and tortillas. However, one of the volunteers handed me a gift card. There was no value printed on the card but I hoped it would be enough to buy my grandchildren a few small gifts. Imagine my surprise when I went to the store and found out the card was worth $500. The unexpected money allowed me to buy Christmas presents for my grandchildren and enough groceries to fill my pantry. Feeling encouraged, I signed up for a call center training program and will begin working in less than a month.

Someone once told me that God always provides. Up until the day I walked into the food pantry, I had begun to doubt that. However, that day, He not only provided, He did it in a way that changed my life. If it had not been for the volunteer and her generous gift, my Christmas would have been quite different. I wouldn't have a full pantry and I wouldn't be looking forward to starting a *career and earning a living and my future wouldn't look as good as it does now. I thank that volunteer, the food pantry and all the people who reach out to help people in need. God bless you all and have a wonderful new year — I know I will.*

A grateful friend

Most times, we don't learn the end results of our seemingly random acts of kindness, but once in a while, we do. Either way, our reward comes not from the knowing but from the doing.

~Margaret M. Nava

Snow Angel

*The best way to find yourself, is to lose
yourself in the service of others.*
~Mahatma Gandhi

I couldn't believe it was snowing. It never snowed in Ohio this early. When I first drove to Cincinnati to stay with my friends for Thanksgiving, we were having perfectly warm fall weather. Now I was heading into what would become known as the Blizzard of 1977.

My friends begged me to stay a few more days, but I declined. I couldn't remain motionless. It was during the quiet, the stillness, that I felt overwhelmed by emotions, consumed by thoughts of him — Sargent Charles Anderson. My husband. My soul mate and protector, the one and only person who would never leave my side. We had been married only a month before he was taken from me, killed in a helicopter crash during a military training exercise.

I had just passed Columbus, the halfway point between Cleveland and Cincinnati, when the weather turned worse. The flakes joined the land and sky into a blurry white void and my car was skidding all over the highway.

My mind turned inward and I thought of Chuck. He never failed to amaze me. Somehow, he could make any situation right. I wished he was with me, but no matter how much I needed him, he would never be there.

But I still had my son, eight-year-old Sam. I looked at him in the back seat. I needed to find a place to stop. Then, through the white haze, I saw our salvation — a green sign reading "Rest Area." At last, someplace we could wait out the storm.

I pulled in, noticing the car's gas needle nearing empty. It didn't matter as long as we had someplace warm to stay. I parked in the lot and left my son sleeping in the back seat as I went to check inside.

As I trudged through the snow toward the brown pavilion, something felt wrong. There were no lights on. I went to the door, only to find it locked. The only rest stop for miles and we couldn't get in. My heart sank. Whatever strength was holding me together since my husband's death, disappeared. I collapsed into the snow and wept.

That's how he found me. He knelt down and asked, "What's wrong?"

Between sobs, I choked out, "My husband's dead. He died in a helicopter crash."

"Overseas?" he asked.

I nodded weakly.

"I read about it in the newspaper."

I looked up at him in disbelief. How could this man possibly know what I was talking about? Then he added, "I flew helicopters in Vietnam."

Slowly, I regained my composure. He told me he was a truck driver for Fazio's Supermarkets on his way north. He was behind schedule and had to get back on the road, but he asked if there was anything he could do to help. I told him my car couldn't make it through the snow. He suggested I follow behind his rig since the eighteen-wheeler would pack down the snow. It didn't work. My car went off the road before we left the on-ramp.

He climbed out of his cab and forced his way through the snow to my car. He helped me out first, and then turned to retrieve my son. He stopped, momentarily startled.

"He has crutches?" he asked in disbelief. Sam was temporarily using crutches as the result of a sprained ankle.

His bewilderment lasted only a moment as he lifted Sam from the car and carried him to his truck. He drove us to the nearest hotel.

He pulled up to the hotel's front door, stopping right in front of a sign that read, "No Semi-Trailer Trucks." After Sam and I were settled in our room, he turned to leave, reminding me he had a schedule to keep. I don't know why he decided to pull over at that rest stop when he did, where he came from, or how he knew of my husband's death. I only know that at the moment I needed him most, somehow, it seemed like my husband was still watching over me. I thanked the truck driver for all he had done for us, but there just didn't seem to be words to say how truly grateful I was.

As he opened the door to leave, he hesitated. Turning, he looked at me and said, "I never knew why I got out of Vietnam alive. But now I know — it was so I could be here tonight to help you." He closed the door and I never saw him again.

~Gloria Anderson Goss

Just When I Needed It

Give yourself entirely to those around you. Be
generous with your blessings. A kind gesture can
reach a wound that only compassion can heal.
~Steve Maraboli, Life, the Truth,
and Being Free

"Look, Mommy, look!" Jimmy had a hopeful smile. He was holding a plastic package filled with green army men. "Can I buy these, please?" I returned his sweet smile and told him that he could put his treasure in the shopping cart along with the food and other necessities that we were buying. I watched as all three of my children—Steven, age eleven; Ana, age eight; and Jimmy, age five—chose a few small items to keep them occupied in the car during our long ride from Georgia to New Hampshire.

My heart ached, even as they happily picked out their new toys and activity books. This trip was monumental, and I was both excited and terrified. After divorcing my husband of sixteen years, I was taking the children back home to my family.

The children were happily chattering about their new toys as we stood in the checkout line. As I watched our purchases add up on the register, I started to get nervous. It was obvious that the running total I had been calculating as we shopped was wrong. We would have to put back all the children's toys and activity books.

Tears were clouding my eyes as I told the children I wouldn't be able to treat them after all. They didn't say a word, but their crestfallen faces broke my heart. Ana ran her hand down her pony's mane one last time before she removed it from the conveyor belt. My children were losing their father, their friends, their home, and even their cat.

Suddenly, a petite woman with dark brown hair and two young children of her own stepped in front of me. Because of my tears, I was barely able to see the forty dollars she placed in my hand. When I realized what she was offering, I started to protest, but she put her hands over mine and said, "I've been in your shoes before. Please buy those things for your children."

At that moment, I felt her sincerity and it comforted me deeply. I cried once more, but this time it was tears of relief. I hadn't realized how much strain and loneliness I had been feeling, and how worried I was about the children's loss. This woman may have been human, but, to me, she was an angel.

All I could do was thank her over and over. After I paid the cashier, I tried to give this generous woman the change, but she refused to take it. Her kindness overwhelmed me.

That good-hearted woman had no idea that she changed my life that day. From that point forward, I hoped for the chance to do the same for someone else one day when I could.

Then one day the children and I were shopping in Walmart. We found ourselves in line behind a mom whose infant was sleeping in a car seat in her shopping cart. She was in the same pickle I had been in: she had more items than cash and she was struggling to choose what to buy. My heart went out to her and I knew I wanted to help. When I saw that one thing she had to give up was a bag of red apples, something so simple and nourishing, I didn't waste a moment.

Steven was ahead of me in line, so I asked him to tap her gently on the arm. When she turned I said, "If you will allow me, I'd really be happy to pay for your order."

She stared at me for a moment in disbelief. Then her eyes widened and she replied, "All of it?"

I smiled and answered, "Yes, because a few years ago I was in need and someone did the same for me. Please let me do this for you."

Still looking shocked, she thanked me and added

her discarded things back onto the conveyor belt. I could see the weight lift from her shoulders and it brought me such joy. After it was paid for and bagged, the young mother gave us a big smile and another heartfelt thank-you. She left the store with a spring in her step that day. My children and I had quite a bit of springiness, too, along with a strong desire to continue paying it forward.

~Jennifer Zink

The Driver's License

*If we have the opportunity to be generous with
our hearts, we have no idea of the depth
and breadth of love's reach.*
~Margaret Cho

I t had been a typical busy day at Frank Family Vineyards in Napa Valley. As I was closing up I noticed a driver's license in the cash register drawer. There was a note with it explaining that someone had found it in the women's restroom.

I had almost finished counting the register receipts when the phone rang. It was a woman named Christine Lewis, and she was the mother of the young woman who had left her driver's license behind. She said they were returning to San Francisco and had just started across the Golden Gate Bridge when her daughter realized she had left it. She was flying back to New York the next morning at 6:30 a.m. and needed her driver's license to board the plane.

Christine said they were meeting friends whom they hadn't seen for several years for dinner in San Francisco. She asked if there was anyway I could hide the driver's license on the property; they would drive all the way back up to Napa after dinner to retrieve it.

I could have left the license under the front door mat of the tasting room, but I thought about what a bad way it would be for them to end their day after having such a great experience here in Napa Valley. And then I asked, "Where are you staying in San Francisco? I don't have anything planned tonight. Go ahead and meet your friends for dinner. I will put your daughter's license in an envelope and leave it at the front desk of your hotel."

Christine asked me where I lived. When I told

her that I lived ten minutes from the winery she was surprised. After all, San Francisco is an hour and a half away, so it would be a three-hour round trip.

The phone was silent and then she asked, "You would do that?"

I said, "Sure, I don't have anything planned tonight." I hung up the phone and a few minutes later it rang again. It was Christine asking if there was someplace they could meet me halfway. I told her not to worry about it. They should just meet their friends.

I locked up the building, stopped at my house to change my clothes, and then started my drive to San Francisco. I had just passed Rutherford Grill when my cell phone rang. It was my good friend, Babs. She wanted to know if I would like to go to dinner. I told her, "I would love to go to dinner!"

Babs said, "Where do you want to go?"

I said, "How about the City?"

She said, "The City, you mean San Francisco, on a Thursday night?"

I told her I was driving there to drop off someone's driver's license and if she wanted to go with me, I would turn around and pick her up in St. Helena and I would explain everything to her on our way.

When Babs and I were almost to San Francisco, Christine called and asked if we would come by the restaurant where they were eating dinner instead of dropping off the license at their hotel. They wanted to thank me personally and her husband wanted to pay me for my gas. I told her I would stop by the restaurant, but I absolutely would not take any money.

When Babs and I walked into the restaurant, almost everyone started clapping. A young woman ran up and hugged me. I instantly recognized her from the picture on the license. The looks on their faces were priceless and I received lots of hugs. The husband wanted to pay me and again I declined. He then insisted on buying dinner for us.

After the family left, Babs and I sat at our table sipping wine. She was quiet for a few minutes and then she told me that this restaurant had a special meaning for her. Her oldest son, who had passed away a few years earlier, had his graduation dinner there. It was bittersweet for her, but she was glad to be there again. What a coincidence, that we had ended up in this restaurant that held special memories for her. It was a fitting end to a beautiful day.

~Pamela Schock

Meet Our Contributors

Piper Dellums is an author, public and inspirational speaker, inter- national victims advocate, member of the United Nations delegate commission on the status of women, lm producer, mother of two, environmentalist, international human rights and dignities activist, and survivor. She received degrees from UC Berkeley and New York University.

Alice Faye Duncan writes for children and adults. Her picture book, *Honey Baby Sugar Child*, is a mother's bouncing love song dedicated to children everywhere. Duncan's adult book, *Hello Sunshine*, is a handy guide to help workers de-stress on busy or cloudy days. Learn more at alicefayeduncan.com and read her blog at uncloudyday.com.

Melissa Edmondson is proud to have her fth story published in the *Chicken Soup for the Soul* series. She is the author of a book of essays entitled *Lessons Abound* and a book of original poetry entitled *Searching for Home: The Poetic Musings of a Wanderer*. She lives in the North Carolina mountains with her husband and four teenage children.

Skye Galvas joined the Air Force from a homeless shelter in 2010. Now a civilian, she lives with her family in Salt Lake City and works as a business consultant, advocate and speaker. She plans to release her book *Alacrity* in 2017. E-mail her at skyegalvas@gmail.com and read her blog at skyegalvas.com.

Gloria Anderson Goss is a member of Gold Star

Wives and a watercolor artist living in Central Pennsylvania with her husband Jeff. Her article, "Why Helicopters Don't Fly and Young Men Die" was published in the *Congressional Record* on June 20, 1984.

Carol Graham is an award-winning author of *Battered Hope*, talk show host for "Never Ever Give Up Hope," international keynote speaker, business owner, and certi ed health coach. Carol has ve grandchil- dren and has rescued over thirty dogs. Her goal is to share hope and encouragement. E-mail her at batteredhope@gmail. com.

Margaret Nava writes from her home in New Mexico where the skies are always blue and the chilis red hot. In addition to her stories in the *Chicken Soup for the Soul* series, she has authored six books and written numerous articles for inspirational and Christian living publications.

Nan Rockey lives in Bloomington, IN, with her writer husband and her non-writer dog. They enjoy long walks in the woods and eating cheesecake when they aren't in the woods.

Lindy Schneider, author, playwright, and artist has been featured on the TV show *Inside Edition*. Her watercolors appear on Amazon's best-selling notecards. She is co-author and illustrator of the children's book *Star fish on the Beach*. See her artwork at peakspublishing.com or search her name on Amazon.com.

Pamela Schock has two children and four grandchildren. She loves to travel and garden. After working for almost a decade in the Napa Valley wine industry, Pam is writing *Tales From the Tasting Room*, a collection of heartwarming and humorous short stories about her encounters in the tasting room. E-mail her at pamelitatales@aol.com.

Jennifer Zink received her Bachelor of Arts degree from Rowan University, Glassboro, NJ, in 2012. She is married with three children: Mike, age twenty; Kimmy, age eighteen; and Daniel, age sixteen. Jen loves to read and write, spend time with her family, and travel.

Meet Amy Newmark

Amy Newmark is the best-selling author, editor-in-chief, and publisher of the *Chicken Soup for the Soul* book series. Since 2008, she has published 140 new books, most of them national bestsellers in the U.S. and Canada, more than doubling the number of Chicken Soup for the Soul titles in print today. She is also the author of *Simply Happy*, a crash course in Chicken Soup for the Soul advice and wisdom that is filled with easy-to-implement, practical tips for having a better life.

Amy is credited with revitalizing the Chicken

Soup for the Soul brand, which has been a publishing industry phenomenon since the first book came out in 1993. By compiling inspirational and aspirational true stories curated from ordinary people who have had extraordinary experiences, Amy has kept the twenty-four-year-old Chicken Soup for the Soul brand fresh and relevant.

Amy graduated *magna cum laude* from Harvard University where she majored in Portuguese and minored in French. She then embarked on a three-decade career as a Wall Street analyst, a hedge fund manager, and a corporate executive in the technology field. She is a Chartered Financial Analyst.

Her return to literary pursuits was inevitable, as her honors thesis in college involved traveling throughout Brazil's impoverished northeast region, collecting stories from regular people. She is delighted to have come full circle in her writing career — from collecting stories "from the people" in Brazil as a twenty-year-old to, three decades later, collecting stories "from the people" for Chicken Soup for the Soul.

When Amy and her husband Bill, the CEO of Chicken Soup for the Soul, are not working, they are visiting their four grown children.

Follow Amy on Twitter @amynewmark. Listen to her free daily podcast, The Chicken Soup for the Soul Podcast, at www.chickensoup.podbean.com, or find it on iTunes, the Podcasts app on iPhone, or on your favorite podcast app on other devices.

Chicken Soup
for the Soul

Changing lives one story at a time®
www.chickensoup.com